MW00617413

FOLLOW YOU ANYWHERE

22 LITTLE LESSONS FOR TEAM LEADERS

kyleSEXTON

Follow You Anywhere –
22 Little Lessons for Team Leaders

First Edition | ISBN: 978-0-9835703-5-6

Published by IncPlant – *Where Ideas Go to Grow*
Salem, Oregon | KyleSexton.com

Unattributed quotations are by Kyle Sexton
Design and composition by Kyle Sexton
Cover design by Kyle Sexton
Cover Artwork Copyright © iStock by danleap

For bulk discounts or other resources,
visit kylesexton.com or call 888-899-8374

Dedicated to the memory of

Michael T. McLaran

Minister of Excellence
to a tribe that grows
even after his passing

CONTENTS

Foreword by Chris McLaran........................ 6

Introduction by Kyle Sexton........................ 8

Team 10

Initiative 12

Firing 14

Dignity..16

Blame 18

Annual Review..20

Discipline 22

Teach – by Scott Sadler 24

Diplomacy...26

Promises 28

Integrity 30

Patience 32

Listen – by Tom Hoffert 34

Focus – by Greg Astley..................................36

Silence...38

Champion 40

Excellence 42

Trust 44

Love...46

Faith..48

McLaranism 50

About Mike McLaran......................................52

Acknowledgements 54

BONUS: Leave It Better Than You Found It 55

About Kyle Sexton..56

FOREWORD

When I was growing up, we had an old skinny inch thick piece of plywood from the 1970's that my dad called a weight bench in our garage. Its padding consisted of a black vinyl covering and old sweat. You would need to lay down two towels on the bench or else you could easily chip your shoulder blade.

Dad always wanted to push me to my limit. He would push me to do just one more press. After I would struggle to push the bar all the way up, he would say, "Just one more," and again, "Just one more."

I can still see him standing behind me as gravity would push the bar down toward my chest. He would encourage me saying, "Push it!" "You can do it!" I would throw everything I had into pushing the weight up.

Half way up, I could feel my arms start to shake as exhaustion set in. I would feel myself start to doubt that I could make it all the way up.

I can still hear him say, "You can do it... Push!" Just when I would feel like the weight was too heavy, he would just stick his hand out and gently touch the bar and I could push the weight up.

I often think about how my dad encouraged me to do my very best. I also think that his role in my life helped me be my very best. It wasn't just his hand under the bar that gave me the confidence to push up the weight. What really mattered was him encouraging me to do something I wouldn't have even tried to do on my own. In fact, without his encouragement there would be no story to tell or lesson to learn. He saw my potential and cheered me to reach for it.

Likewise, our roles as leaders should at times take the form of a spotter. We should be encouraging each other to reach our potential, spotting excellence and gently raising the bar. Let these (McLaranisms) remind you of one of the greatest motivators that ever lived.

Follow You Anywhere honors my father by preserving the words and phrases that capture the true heart of leadership. I hope his words push you to become a better leader, mentor and friend.

A spotter of excellence, Kyle Sexton has masterfully captured the brilliant blend of my dad's wisdom and encouragement.

Christopher J. McLaran

INTRODUCTION

If you're lucky, you will meet someone who embodies a servant leader in your lifetime. I was able to work down the hall from such a person for over a decade. To say it was transformative would be the understatement of my life.

Like all of us who accomplish something, you have people who helped you along the way. *Help* might not be the right term. Maybe the right word is *mentor*, *coach*, *nurture*, or *choose*. It was all of these for me.

I would follow you anywhere. I never said it out loud to my hero but it is the phrase that is branded on my heart like a scar from an iron. If you think that seems painful, you're right. He was taken from us at the end of March, 2013.

As I looked around at the memorial of Mike McLaran, I sat in disbelief at the number of people who claimed to have received his best: 900 people, maybe a thousand.

I must introduce you to McLaranism. What began as a list or set of attributes on a cathartic blog post in the early hours of March 31, 2013, has become a tribe.

"I am a talker," claims Anissa Starnes. "I talk a lot, so it hit me like a ton of bricks when I read *Listen with your eyes and your ears will work better*. Since the day I read that it has changed me. It has helped me be a better wife, daughter, step-mother, manager and leader."

Even though Anissa never met the inspiration for this collection, she has learned—like so many others—some valuable lessons from the McLaranisms.

"Isn't it a wonderful thing," she adds, "that someone that we never met can make such a difference in our lives?"

What I love about Mike McLaran is that he was the human embodiment of a brand that many of us aspire to be. He is servant leadership exemplified.

I'm no leadership expert. My role in this book is that of a narrator. Many others contributed to this project. In some cases, entire sections are narrated by someone other than me, and noted appropriately. You will be directed to discover other contributions at the end of the book.

I didn't invent the McLaranisms; Mike did. I was there to document them. My life's work is to teach others what I learned from gurus like Mike.

1

TEAM

NO ONE CAN BE GREAT AT THEIR ROLE · IF EVERYONE ISN'T GREAT AT THEIR ROLE ·

The key aspect of *Team* is that everybody has a role, but no role is more important than any other role. In baseball and softball, the pitcher's record depends on how well his or her defensive teammates play their positions. Sure, the pitcher gets a lot of attention, but it's the total defense that contributes to any good pitcher's dominating statistics.

No one can be great at their job if everyone isn't great at their job. Any role can be critical to the goal of the organization at any time. Over the life of any company, you can bet that the most random role can make or break the organization given the right set of circumstances.

The team is never just about the people in the spotlight. Those in the most visible roles of your team are made better by those in support roles, and also by those utility players who can step in and step up to a role and pick up where you left off.

Next one up isn't just a team-building strategy. It's also valuable for sun-setting and legacy planning. Who do you have on your team ready to step in for you? More importantly, for which roles in your organization are you prepared to fill in when needed?

Team is not a vertical alignment, nor is it horizontal. The leader you follow is willing and able to do your job in support of the team.

2

The best ideas in your organization most likely won't come from you. They come from your teammates. They come from your customers. And they come from your former customers.

No matter the source, your organization's best asset is not the idea. Your best asset is initiative. Who, on your team, hits the *go* button?

Before your team even has an opportunity to get their fingerprints on what's next, someone has to initiate the idea.

If your organization is a vacuum for suggestions, or a black hole of innovation, don't expect your fans to make you better.

Fast-moving teams attract fast-moving innovations. Setting aside shiny objects that don't add value or efficiency to your organization, your company's greatest accomplishments just might start with a suggestion from a client, or a criticism of a former customer.

When the idea hits your desk, how will you reward it? Who on your team is best equipped to vet it?

You need other people to start things and take risks. When someone brings you a worthwhile initiative, it's your support that can deliver the resulting service or efficiency to your company and community.

3

Firing

Employees

FAILURE IN HIRING

FAILURE TO ALIGN

Firing might be good therapy for a fast-moving industrialist, but this message is for small businesses that move fast on a regional level. The famous firings made famous by television shows like *The Apprentice* make a mockery of business for those of us who care about culture, community and social enterprise.

When a manager makes a poor hiring decision, she has two choices. Fast correction will be perceived by your team as an annulment, where a prolonged suffering may result in a lengthy, painful divorce.

Other times, your team suffers from misalignment. I work with many organizations like this. In a small organization, the position someone is hired for isn't always the role in which they will thrive.

Assessing the strengths of people is part art, part science. In order to do this well, you should first acknowledge that your brain works differently than everyone else's.

In our new economy, there are some new best-practices. These include annual team testing for strengths, compatibilities, and efficiencies. Try a rotation of strength assessments like D-I-S-C, Kolbe Corp and Sally Hogshead.

Great leaders are constantly assessing the strengths and gaps of their team. You may discover new ways to work together more efficiently.

4

TAKE THE

Dignity

preserve it

HIGH ROAD

Man did I goof. I missed a meeting. Turns out, it was an important meeting. (Aren't they all?)

The dignity-preserving leader can either chew me out (adding insult to injury) or use it as a coaching moment.

The chew-out is deserved, sure, but I was already beating myself up. So imagine my surprise when my coach didn't even mention it. But wait, there was this hallway conversation.

Coach: "Were you able to follow up with the folks from your missed meeting and make it right? The reason I ask is that I've received some feedback that it has generated some chatter which will affect your own personal credibility, which is something only you can manage."

The careful choice of words in this statement is not just coaching; it is dignified and looking out for me. It puts a future context to the issue which occurred in the past.

Deal with issues over personalities. Next time you are presented with a coaching moment, ask yourself how you can make sure the critical information is presented so the issue can be corrected without making the other party feel defensive.

Dignity is what you preserve in others when you refuse to take anything but the high road.

5

What is blame doing on this list? It's such a negative word. Here's why: Blame is something a leader takes for his or her team even if—or especially if—they had nothing to do with the leader.

Never assign blame to somebody else. Publicly give credit and take blame. Privately correct and discipline.

This provides a safe place for your team to work, and makes it very clear for whom they work. Your team will feel safe to take risks for the betterment of the organization with a leader who puts their name and reputation on the line for the team.

A protective leader gives her team all the tools that they need to be successful. When you have tools and a safe place, you have an environment more conducive to trying new things and new ways to serve your clients.

Having worked in an environment like this for a decade, it was exhilarating to go to work in a place where I had permission to fail, which is completely different than being a failure.

This is a manageable lesson one-to-one, but team dynamics are different. If someone is put on the spot in a group, blame can be a natural flinch, albeit an ugly one. Understanding this will help you lead discussions where information is presented in a way to prevent blame from infecting your team dynamic.

6

★ The ★

McLARAN

ANNUAL REVIEW

Do you still love what you do?

★ ★

WHERE DO YOU WANT TO BE IN FIVE YEARS?

★ ★

How can I help you get there?

Reviewing job performance makes people anxious. Many of us flinch at the idea of planned criticism.

But what if your boss used this to help you dream? That's the performance review I had on a regular basis for 10 years.

Do you still love what you do here? What do you want to be doing in five years? How can I help?

What a selfless gift. When most of us get a hold of someone with a particular set of skills that we don't want to lose, our tendency might be to shield them from other opportunities.

This annual review approach builds trust and reinforces that coaching happens at the time and place needed for the greatest impact.

It seems contradictory to ask about dreams at the risk of the dream not including you.

As a marketing strategist, I'm keenly aware of the emotional nature of dreams and wishes. Buying decisions are also of an emotional nature. Through this lens, consider the goal of the annual review approach to get buy-in and renew the commitment from the team member to the organization.

7

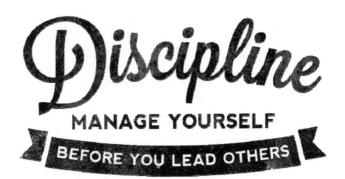

Discipline

MANAGE YOURSELF
BEFORE YOU LEAD OTHERS

You can't lead others if you can't first manage your own life. If you can't discipline yourself, no one will follow you anywhere.

Discipline means having standards for yourself and your team. It means consequences when targets are missed.

Discipline manifests itself in your time management—or mismanagement. At the end of the day, the work you don't finish will still be there tomorrow.

Business will take up as much time as you allow. What are you missing out on today that will not be there tomorrow? Do that instead.

8

Contributed by Scott Sadler

Giving advice does not necessarily make a teaching opportunity. Teaching is accepted when it is presented by someone you trust, whether it's at the office or talking about life over a beer.

Many influential moments can come out of those conversations. The impact of thoughtful advice can have a daily impact on your life and business.

As a fast-paced entrepreneur, I was once facing a particular challenge. In one of our end-of-the-day conversations, Mike suggested I slow down before I take action, become an astute observer and take notes.

"If you observe things from different angles, the resources you need will be apparent," he shared.

His suggestion became a way of life for me. My life flows simply and I'm grateful for the seeds that have become my roots today.

Months later, the roles were reversed. It made me swell with pride to be able to offer my insights to my friend and trusted advisor who had offered so many of his insights to me.

9

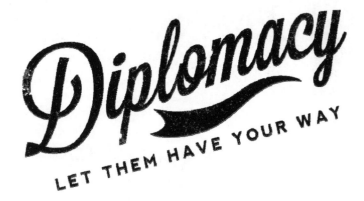

Diplomacy

LET THEM HAVE YOUR WAY

Diplomacy is the art of letting someone else have your way.

Think about that for a moment. Consider how many times you have gone into a meeting with the intent to cut to the chase. You want to tell the team, *I have this answer and we've got a plan in place.*

Letting someone else have your way plays a huge role in team management, because even when we know the right direction, communicating the solution requires that we also communicate the problem.

But when you're the only member of the team who understands the problem, it's *only* your solution; it's not everybody else's solution.

It can take a longer conversation to talk through a solution that is owned by the team. But when the solution comes out of someone else's mouth, you get to respond with, "I think that's a great idea. What do you think we need to do to align for implementation? And could you explain how you arrived at this solution so we can rally the troops?"

11

Promises

A pleaser's intent tends to write checks they can't cash. If you are a leader who has attracted teammates who get themselves into trouble in this way, make sure you are asking questions about what is realistic in their promises.

This has been a hard lesson for me, personally, since I have a habit of overestimating my role and capacity.

Keep your team from breaking promises by keeping tabs on their capacity, and by challenging their promises in a private setting. Report in groups, but commit one-on-one. This is a subtle, yet meaningful way to share your standards with the organization.

12

Integrity is earned over decades, but it's lost in a careless moment. If you have to tell somebody that you have integrity, you probably don't.

I think it's interesting to look at all the companies that brag about having integrity or having trust. I don't think that a brand or an organization ought to talk about integrity. I believe that your clients and customers have to use words like that to describe them.

As a leader in the office or in the field, integrity is earned by making habits that support promises to others. When personal sacrifices are made to keep a promise to someone, you may be surprised who is watching.

If you're doing work that matters, integrity will help it to matter more.

13

PATIENCE

WORK YOUR PLAN

You just can't rush good leadership. Patience from a great leader can be misleading because they make it look so darn easy. It's not easy, but patience shouldn't be confused with waiting.

Patience is something you look like you have while you are working your plan. Patience is what you look like you have when you are smart enough to block the appropriate time for your priorities.

If you're like me, you sometimes fall into the trap of confusing urgent with important. The urgencies want you to believe they are important, but they just aren't. They are usually urgent for someone else because they chased a squirrel, played with that shiny object over there, procrastinated or otherwise lacked the discipline to get their priorities in order.

My own struggle with patience is tied to a belief that I do my best work under pressure. I was once under the impression that I was one of those dreaded procrastinators. As it turns out, since I struggle with focus and time-related discipline, I have trained myself to respond to the pain of the deadline.

Disciplined people are patient, because they can afford to be. This calmness perpetuates calmness, allowing you to be generous with your time towards your team, family and other leaders.

14

LISTEN WITH YOUR EYES

★ ★

Your ears will work better

Contributed by Tom Hoffert

Critical listening skills and engagement with the people you work with is the foundation to professional communication.

Talk less, listen more is kicked around a lot in leadership training. Real communication occurs when you engage with your audience and genuinely care about the information being presented by the other person(s) in a conversation.

Much of communication is non-verbal. It is about truly focusing on the message and passion behind the information that allows us to make a connection or solution. The best part is that sometimes people just need to share what's on their mind. Be someone with whom people are comfortable sharing information.

Being a good listener doesn't mean you're a "yes person." It means people trust you and value your thoughts.

15

Contributed by Greg Astley

We live in a time where the demand for our attention is constantly being imposed on us: By advertisers, by technology, by others and by ourselves. Sadly, so many people today multi-task or "check-out" of a large group meeting by tweeting, emailing, texting or playing a game under the table.

This lack of respect for the person or persons who are speaking is so prevalent, we think nothing of sitting idly by and watching as someone next to us reaches the next level on Candy Crush or sends another text to a friend about "how boring this meeting is I'm in."

A focused leader will never check her phone or glance at her watch during a meeting or even while having a drink with a friend.

Participating in a meeting means giving your full attention and focus. At the beginning of a meeting, let the other person know how much time you have so you can concentrate on the important issues.

If you have chosen to take the time to meet with someone, to spend any amount of time with them, they deserve your full attention and focus and you should expect the same from them. I have found, happily, the more I practice focusing my attention on someone, the more it is returned with respect and courtesy, benefiting us both.

16

SILENCE

~ IS LOUDER ~

Silence takes much patience and discipline.

You don't have to be the first to speak in order to be heard. Your silence can be the loudest thing in any room.

Any group dynamic has people who are uncomfortable with silence. They feel the need to be heard.

There are those who feel validated most when you ask for their approval. There are others who are most valued when you ask them to bring a solution.

A leader knows when to be silent so that she can put the priority on those she has asked to do the work.

A meeting is never over until somebody—in order to break the loud silence—asks the silent leader, "What do you think?"

17

the
CHAMPION
target on your back

Champion is a title that comes with a target on your back. When you're a champion, everybody wants to take you down.

A championship team expends an extraordinary amount to achieve and an even greater amount to stay there. If you're not a contender, if you're not an organization that bleeds excellence, then you're really not part of the conversation.

It takes high standards and discipline—not for just you and your staff—but for your entire team.

18

Hard to Get

Excellence

Harder to Keep

Excellence is just a little bit more than greatness. It's a hard place to get to and it's even harder to stay there.

Excellence is common among champions. Once you achieve that level of excellence, you can either take time to pat yourself on the back or you can realize that there are other people in your organization you need to bring up along with you.

Part of being a leader of people is sending the recognition along to those who help you get there. This position of humility is good for the culture of the team. It reinforces the value of the hard work—the thankless work—that achieved excellence.

Before taking any credit for the excellence of your team, go back and re-read the very first section of this book.

19

TRUST

HONESTY

encouragement

Trust is something you receive when you give it first. When you receive trust from a credible, charismatic leader you don't take that gift for granted.

Trust is the opposite of uncertainty, doubt and skepticism. Trust is not just about leadership; it's also about management. It's about setting the course and relying on people to do their job so that everybody can elevate to that same position in the end.

Great leaders are positive people who work with facts and truth.

Skeptics do not attract winners. Doubters hesitate. Suspicious people don't believe others because they often lie to themselves.

Trust in other people manifests itself in encouragement, support and confidence.

Bonnie Milletto had expressed a fear of moving forward with her speaking career, and in typical fashion, Mike brought the conversation around to a game called life.

"You have a dream," he said. "Follow it. Do not let the fear of the past or the unknown of the future stop you from moving forward. Will you be the one that sits in the stands and just watches or will you get in the game and make positive things happen? You have a gift. It is useless if you don't share it. Get in the game and make things happen!"

20

When honesty and trust and selflessness are directed at somebody else, you've got love.

Sometimes love is the action that inspires the emotion.

First Knight is a favorite movie of mine. It's full of great stories about love, risk and challenge. King Arthur (played by Sean Connery) says...

> To Lancelot (Richard Gere): "A man who fears nothing is a man who loves nothing; and if you love nothing, what joy is there in your life?"

Love, fear and joy are active emotions, whereas sadness and satisfaction are passive emotions. Emotions are active when they cause or contribute to action.

> To Guinevere (Julia Ormond): "I take the good with the bad, together. I can't love people in slices."

Leaders have accepted their team for their strengths and challenges, and aligned them to maximize strengths and minimize weaknesses.

Leaders give meaning to the work. Meaning is defined by what motivates the role player rather than what motivates the leader. Therefore, a leader understands what motivates each member of their team, and communicates in terms that each team member can understand.

21

faith

"The Christian shoemaker does his duty not by putting little crosses on the shoes, but by making good shoes, because God is interested in good craftsmanship." – Martin Luther

Servant leaders are also interested in good craftsmanship. Craftsmanship is the application of values. Service is a demonstration of values. Culture is defined by values.

Faith is not just about religion or spirituality. The faith of a servant leader is also a function of trusting a positive outcome because of the belief you have in your values and those around you.

Leaders express the greatest anxiety when they don't have faith in the people around them.

Conversely, those leaders who are at peace with their accomplishments feel this way because of great faith in those with whom they choose to surround themselves.

22

You are likely no stranger to servant leadership. You talk about it and you practice it in your organization. Like integrity, if you have to talk about it, maybe you're doing it wrong.

Seth Godin once blogged about the quickest way to get things done and make change:

> *Don't demand authority. Eagerly take responsibility. Relentlessly give credit.*

I instantly recognized this as servant leadership, which also requires that you are willing to do— and are capable of doing—anything you would ask of someone else.

This idea has nothing to do with your vertical position on the organizational chart. When you're the boss you work for those you employ, not the other way around.

It's been said that people don't quit jobs, they quit bosses. When your boss is a servant leader, they selflessly help you out of the nest like a bird teaching her chicks to fly.

Learn these lessons. Teach them to others in an honest and vulnerable way. When you do, don't be surprised that the culture you create attracts high achievers who would follow you anywhere.

ABOUT MIKE McLARAN

Mike McLaran was the founder of McLaran Enterprises, a leadership development firm based in Salem, Oregon. Mike used his experience in business and organizational management to move organizations to new levels of excellence.

For more than sixteen years, Mike served as CEO the Salem Area Chamber of Commerce. Prior to coming to Salem, Mike served as the CEO of the Albany, Oregon Chamber of Commerce where he helped establish the Chamber as a highly respected leadership organization.

Mike was graduated from a six-year program in Organization Management held at UCLA. His degree in business management is from the University of Oregon, where Mike was known as a talented baseball player and fierce competitor.

In 2012, Mike received an honorary doctorate from Corban University.

"He was selected because of his years of service to the Salem community and his reputation as a man of high integrity," said the late Reno Hoff, former president of Corban University. "An honorary doctorate is a way to honor someone who has led a distinguished life and Mike McLaran has done that beyond reproach."

Throughout his career, he earned numerous awards including the Russel E. Pettit Memorial Excellence in Leadership Award in 2007, and the Vern Miller Distinguished Service Award from the City of Salem in 2009.

Mike was an active volunteer within the Salem community and has served with the Salem Hospital board, the Salem Leadership Foundation board and the Cascade Pacific Council of the Boy Scouts of America.

More than accomplishments, Mike was most proud of his family: His daughter Katie, his son Chris, and his wife Diane.

ACKNOWLEDGEMENTS

So many folks helped make this project happen. Thanks to Chelsea Pope, Joy Dickinson, Anissa Starnes, Nathan Knottingham, Bonnie Milletto, Russ Rainwater, Christine Dieker, LeAnn Keim, Ed Bock, Jessica Chambers, Debra Herring, Bry Taylor, Karin Holton, Kathy Goss, Greg Astley, Brent Neilsen, Scott Sadler, Sharron Seideman, Dick Seideman, Carole Reynolds, Dan Farrington, Lisa Franceschi-Campbell, Michael Duane Brown, Madeline Nowell, Nick Williams, Jason Brandt, Myron Musick, Cori Pratt, Erin Molyneaux and Dick Withnell.

Thank you, Wyatt, for your support and faith in me. Thank you, Lindsey, for your encouragement and devotion.

Thank you, Gerry Frank, for continuing to be a rock for servant leaders and pilgrims alike.

Thank you, Tom Hoffert, for being willing to make hard phone calls and having high expectations.

Thanks to Chuck and Kathy McLaran for being the parents of McLaranism.

Special thanks to Chris McLaran. This project couldn't happen without you putting your hand under the bar for me.

LEAVE IT BETTER
THAN YOU FOUND IT

If you've read this far, you deserve a bonus. At least a handful of times during this project, the lizard brain had gotten the better of me.

Who am I to put my name on this?

I'm just a guy from down the hall. I'm one of many in a tribe who learned, and has continued to learn. The fact is, if our teacher hadn't been called up to the big leagues, we might not have accepted the next role.

What follows is a compilation of contributions from those who watched, practiced, and have accepted the next role.

View the bonus content on your web browser at http://bonus.mclaranism.com.

ABOUT KYLE SEXTON

Photo by Kris Stalnaker

Kyle Sexton is an award-winning marketing strategist and international speaker on the topics of membership development, marketing and innovation. He was recognized by *Chamber Executive* magazine as one of the most influential innovators in his industry.

Kyle is the chamber of commerce industry's foremost authority on membership tiers, and coaches organizations through their transition from a traditional dues method to a progressive tiered-investment model.

Kyle lives in Salem, Oregon, with his son, Wyatt.

Made in the USA
Middletown, DE
27 July 2019